I CAN BE A
FATHER

By Patrick Clinton

Prepared under the direction of Robert Hillerich, Ph.D.

CHILDRENS PRESS ®

CHICAGO

Library of Congress Cataloging-in-Publication Data

Clinton, Patrick.
  I can be a father / by Patrick Clinton.
     p.   cm.
  Includes index.
  Summary: Describes how fathers provide for, take care
of, and teach their children.
  ISBN O-516-O19O4-X
  1. Fathers—Juvenile literature.   2. Father and child—
Juvenile literature.   [1. Fathers.   2. Father and
child.] I. Title.
HQ756.C56   1988   88-11749
306.8'742—dc19   CIP
                                                   AC

Childrens Press®, Chicago
Copyright ©1989 by Regensteiner Publishing Enterprises, Inc.
All rights reserved. Published simultaneously in Canada.
Printed in the United States of America.
1 2 3 4 5 6 7 8 9 1O R 98 97 96 95 94 93 92 91 90 89

PICTURE DICTIONARY

farm

crops

country

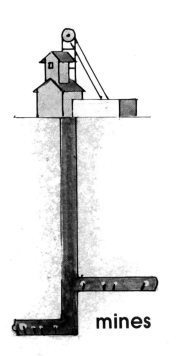

mines

city

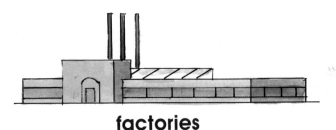

factories

teach

learn

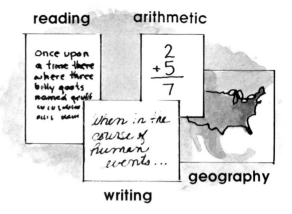

reading

arithmetic

$$\begin{array}{r} 2 \\ + 5 \\ \hline 7 \end{array}$$

geography

writing

business

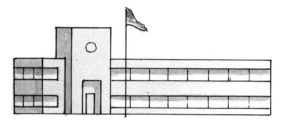

school

shelter

Many years ago children and adults spent their days doing the same things.

farm

crops

country

Long ago most people
thought that children and
adults were about the
same. They played the
same games. They spent
their days in the same
places. If they lived in the
country, they worked on
the farm. They took care of
the animals and raised
crops. If they lived in the
city, they worked in
crowded houses that were
part home and part business.

city

business

Boys worked with their fathers (left) and girls worked with their mothers (right).

Boys worked with their fathers. Girls worked with their mothers. When they were only seven or eight years old, some children were sent to work for other people. There they learned to do the work they would do for the rest of their life.

Instead of going to school, children were sent to work.

They might learn to catch fish or make shoes or weave cloth. Few children went to school.

No one worried about  children. Most people thought children were just tiny adults.

school

Childhood is a special time for learning.

That's not what people
think today. Today no one
thinks children are workers.
Today people think
childhood is a special time
for learning and growing. In
most countries, children

In school, children learn about the world.

aren't sent to work. They don't work in factories or mines. Instead, fathers and mothers send their children to school. There they learn things they will need to know when they are grown up.

factories

mines

Schools do part of the work of raising a child. But there is still plenty of work for a mother and father.

And what does a father do? Well, different parents do things in different ways. But almost all fathers help do three things for their children: provide for them, care for them, and teach them.

Fathers care for their children (top),
teach them (bottom left),
and provide for them (bottom right).

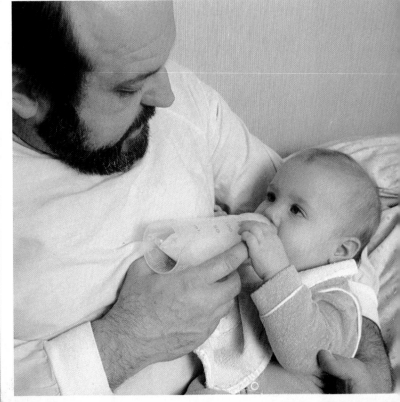

Some fathers still work with their children on family farms.

To provide for a family means to get the food and clothing and shelter the family needs to live. Long ago most families built their own shelters. They raised or hunted for food. They also

shelter

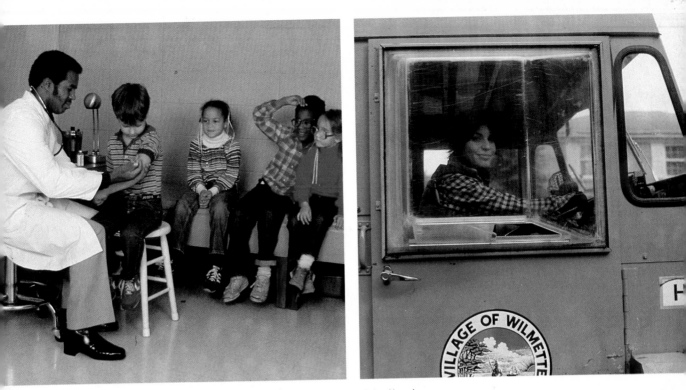

Most fathers, and many mothers, have jobs outside the home.

made their own clothes—
and sometimes even their
own cloth. Today most
families buy their food and
clothing. And that means
that someone needs to earn
money. Most fathers—and
many mothers—have jobs.

13

Fathers work so they can earn money to take care of their families.

A father may drive a truck or build houses or sell things in a store. A father loves his children and wants to take care of them, and that is his most important reason for working.

Fathers are very proud of their families.

People who have jobs can't always be home. Most fathers are out of the house all day long at a factory or in an office. Some, like sailors and soldiers, are away for months at a time.

Many fathers work in offices.

But they're still fathers. They keep in touch with their families by telephone and letters. Fathers help make decisions and give advice. They help care for their families.

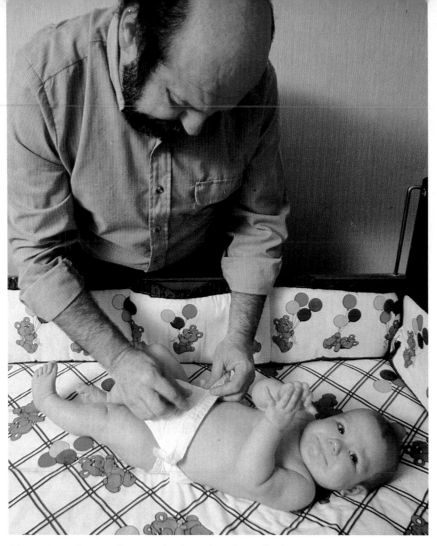

Changing diapers is a part of caring for a baby.

Caring for a family means many different things. It can mean cooking and cleaning or changing diapers. It can mean fixing a leaky faucet

Family chores are fun to do together.

or building a new fence—
or even playing a game.
It can mean taking care
of a hurt knee or making
someone feel better after
something bad has
happened.

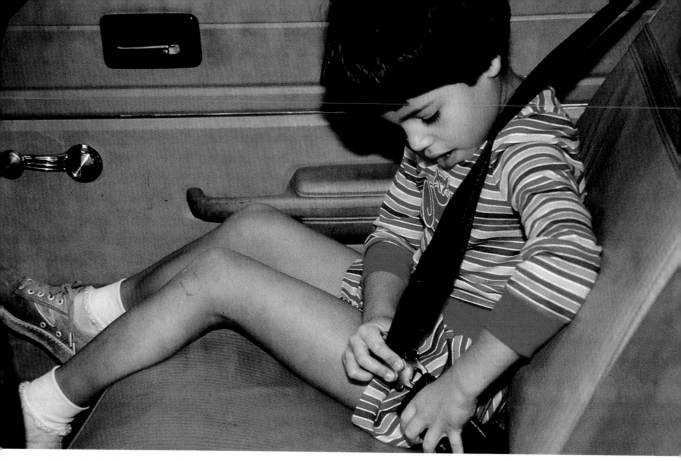

Rules help keep us safe.

One of the most important
ways fathers take care
of their children is by
making rules. Rules have
many different purposes.
*Always wear your seat belt
in the car,* is a rule for

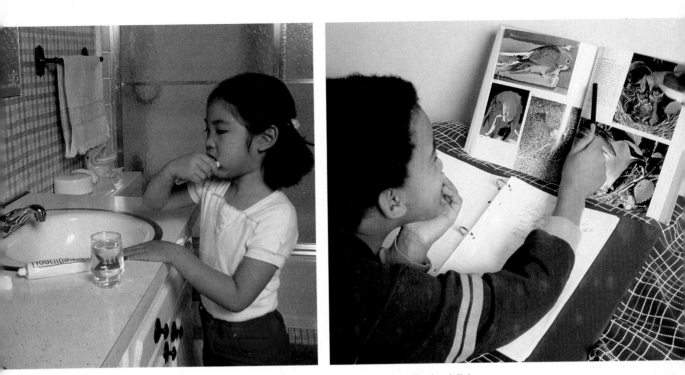

Fathers and mothers make rules because they care for their children.

safety. *Brush your teeth before going to bed*, is a rule to keep a child healthy. *Always do your homework*, is a rule to make sure children learn what they'll need to know in life.

Fathers teach their children many things.

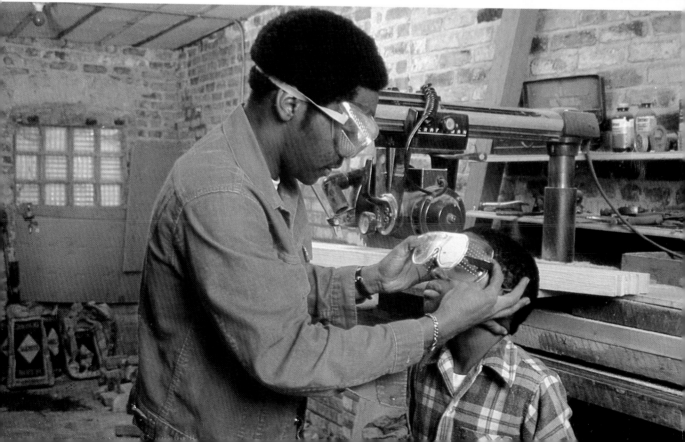

Learning is an important part of being a child. Teaching is an important part of being a father.

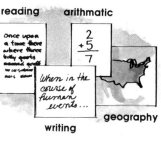

reading   arithmatic

writing   geography

Schools teach many things—reading, writing, arithmetic, and geography. But that leaves many things for a father to teach. A

teach

learn

father starts teaching when his children are little babies. He never stops teaching.

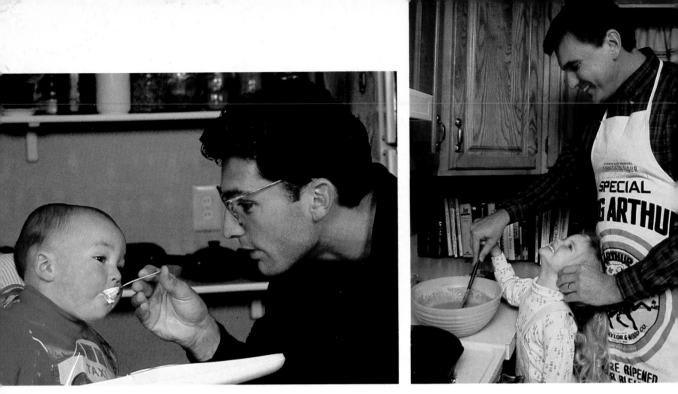

Fathers feed their children (left) and teach them how to cook (right).

What does a father
teach? He might teach a
baby to walk and talk, to
eat with a spoon, or to play.
He might teach a boy or girl
to play games, to throw a
ball, or cook, or paint, or
work with tools. When his

As children grow up, fathers teach them new skills.

children are teenagers, a
father might teach them
to drive a car, or sail a
boat, or work at a job. At
every age, a father tries
to teach the difference
between right and wrong.
He tries to show his
children the best way
he knows to live.

Fathers work at many different jobs.

There's not just one way
to be a father. In many
families the father earns a
paycheck, and the mother
stays home with the
children. In some families it's
the other way around. The

Sometimes a father stays home while the mother goes to work.

father stays home to cook and clean, while the mother goes to work. Some fathers raise their children alone. Some fathers adopt other people's children and raise

27

Fathers have the best job in the world.

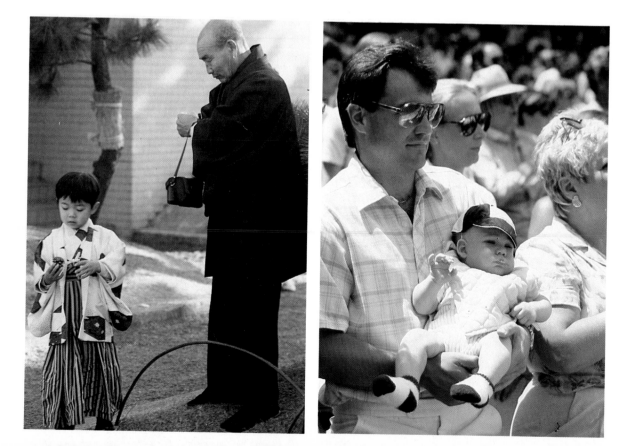

them. A man who raises and loves and cares for a child is called that child's father, no matter who the birth father is.

Fathers have one thing in common. Fathers love their children and want them to grow to be healthy and happy. Taking care of children is a big job, but most fathers think it's the best job in the world.

WORDS YOU SHOULD KNOW

adopt(uh • DOPT) — bring into a family through legal steps someone else's child and raise as one's own

adult — a person who has reached legal age

advice(ad • VYCE) — helpful suggestion

crops(CRAHPS) — vegetables or grain gathered or growing on a farm

decision(dih • SIH • jun) — the settlement reached at making up one's mind

earn(ERN) — to be paid in return for work or service

factory(FAK • tor • ee) — a building where things are made to be sold, such as clothing, food items, furnishings, tools

learning(LER • ning) — beginning to understand through instruction and experience

mines(MYNES) — underground areas containing precious metals, minerals, rocks, or gems

office(AWF • iss) — a room, or building, where people work for a business or profession

parents(PAIR • ents) — a person's father and mother; a male and a female who have a child or children

plenty(PLEN • tee) — a large amount, often more than enough

provide(pro • VYDE) — to afford care, feeding, and shelter

purposes(PER • puhsses) — desired results, aims

reason(REE • zun) — the cause or thing that explains a belief or action

rules(ROOLZ) — a statement of proper conduct for a group, decided by its governing body

safety(SAIF • tee) — freedom from danger or evil

shelter(SHEL • ter) — housing; a home; protection from harm

weave(WEEVE) — to make cloth by passing yarn or threads in one direction over and under those in another direction

worry(WER • ee) — to be troubled or uncertain of outcome

INDEX

INDEX, Continued

PHOTO CREDITS

Click/Chicago, Ltd.:
   © John Anderson—21 (right)
   © Billy E. Barnes—11 (bottom left)
   © Cezus—25 (both photos)
   © John Coletti—26 (right)
   © D.E. Cox—9 (left)
   © John Lawlor—15
   © Carol Lee—24 (right)
   © Norman Mossallem—26 (left)
   © Don Smetzer—14 (right)

The Granger Collection, New York—6 (right),
7 (right)

Historical Pictures Service, Inc.—4 (bottom), 6 (left)

Journalism Services:
   © Paul F. Gero—12 (right)
   © Stephen Green—28 (bottom right)
   © Steve Sumner—12 (left)
   © Jim Zietz—Cover

© Norma Morrison—9 (right), 14 (left), 20, 28 (top),
28 (bottom left)

Nawrocki Stock Photo:
   © Jeff Apoian—16, 27
   © David Bentley—13 (both photos), 21 (left),
   22 (bottom)
   © Melanie Carr—11 (top), 24 (left)
   © Randall Haglund—8
   © Melanie Kaestner—17
   © Bill Renoit—11 (bottom right), 18
   © Sylvia Schlender—19 (left)
   © J. Steere—22 (top right)
   © Les Van—22 (top left)
   © Jim Whitmer—19 (right)

North Wind Picture Archives—4 (top), 7 (left)

ABOUT THE AUTHOR

Patrick Clinton has his master's degree from Northwestern University. He was the managing editor of the *Reader* for eight years and is currently a senior editor at *Chicago* magazine. He lives in Chicago with his wife, Susan, and their two sons.